D0502648

All inquiries should be addressed to:
Barron's Educational Series, Inc.
250 Wireless Boulevard
Hauppauge, New York 11788

International Standard Book No. 0-8120-6087-3

Library of Congress Catalog Card No. 88-927

PRINTED IN THE NETHERLANDS
8901   987654321

Marjolein Bastin

Vera in the Kitchen

Translation by Emilie Boon
Verse by Jean Grasso Fitzpatrick

BARRON'S

New York • Toronto

In our kitchen
     there's a big cookbook.
When we're feeling hungry
     we just take a look.
Little Chick thinks
     that soup's a real treat,
But it's my turn to choose,
     so spaghetti's what we'll eat.

Spaghetti's so delicious
    I could eat it by the ton,
And in front of a mirror
    it's twice as much fun.
"Look!" says Little Doll.
    "You keep dropping it!"
"Don't worry," I reply,
    "I'll pick up every bit."

With so many little
    mouths to feed
Look at all
    the food we need!
I get home from the market
    too tired to think,
So I sit myself down
    with some milk to drink.

Peeling potatoes
     is so much fun,
But the floor is soaking
     when we're done.
Not to worry,
     though, you see—
Little Doll will mop it
     up for me!

Everyone helps
    get the table set.
Are they all hungry?
    Yes, you bet!
To tell you the truth,
    even *I* can't wait.
Little Chick's tomato soup
    is really great!

Making pancakes
    is quite a feat.
They're Little Doll's
    favorite thing to eat.
We always drop some
    on the floor,
But don't worry...
    we can make plenty more!

We're sneaking some sugar—
  that's not *too* bad.
Just a pinch of it
  is all we've had.
Afterward, away
  we'll all be rushing
To give our teeth
  a thorough brushing.

Ladybug has
    her own bowl and cup.
Every morning
    when she wakes up
I fix some oatmeal
    for her to eat,
Then we walk together
    down the street.

When Little Doll has
    something to eat
No one could say
    that she is neat.
It's impossible to
    avoid the mess,
So I tie a big napkin
    over my dress.

Picking berries
    in the woods was fun.
We picked enough
    for everyone!
But it was very silly—
    and I mean *very* —
Not to change our dresses
    before touching a berry.

I love rosehip jam,
don't you?
And all my dollies
love it, too.
We've gathered so many
rosehips today
That my old basket
has worn away.

In the summer we love
a picnic lunch.
We bring along wonderful
things to munch.
Little Chick chirps
with pure delight.
He'd like to eat
everything in sight!